Kudzu Cuisine

**Festive cookery
to delight
the adventurous
and
intrigue the skeptics**

KUDZU
CUISINE

Festive cookery
to delight
the adventurous
and
intrigue the skeptics

Juanitta Baldwin

Suntop Press
A Division of Suntop, Inc.
Kodak, Tennessee 37764
Virginia Beach, Virginia 23462

Printed and bound in the United States of America
First Printing 2000

ISBN 1-880308-23-1

Library of Congress Cataloging-in-Publication Data

Baldwin, Juanitta
    Kudzu cuisine : festive recipes to delight the adventurous and intrigue the skeptics! /
Juanitta Baldwin.
        p. cm.
    ISBN 1-880308-23-1
        1. Cookery (Kudzu) 2. Kudzu. I Title.

TX814.5.K83 B35 2000
641.6--dc21

                                                                99-058618

Table of Contents

Preface IV
Acknowledgments V
About the Author VI
I Met Kudzu One Happy Summer Day VII
Nutrients in Kudzu VIII

Part I
Kudzu Flower Cookery

Part II
Kudzu Leaf and Vine Cookery

Part III
Kudzu Root Cookery

Part IV
Kudzu Vine Powder®

Preface

Kudzu vine grows so prolifically in the Southeastern United States that it is a serious environmental problem. Many persons know that kudzu has medicinal properties but do not know it is a human food. This is due in large measure to the fact that most news releases and books tout kudzu to control soil erosion, and as an animal feed.

More Americans are eating kudzu than anyone would have believed twenty years ago. *Kudzu Cuisine* is a cookbook for those who may wish to read about this new development, or try kudzu in some form. Stories and information about kudzu are entwined within the recipe pages for a change of reading pace. Even if you never cook or eat a kudzu dish, you can marvel at those of us who do, perhaps as I marvel at persons who salivate at the site of raw fish or whale blubber.

Dr. Robert Tanner of Vanderbilt University has conducted many scientific studies on kudzu. He tells us that kudzu has saved the Japanese from famine in times gone by. When famine struck, the Japanese would go to the kudzu patches and survive by eating it. In the event of a nuclear disaster, kudzu may save the people of the South, because kudzu roots grow deeper in the soil than nuclear radiation is known to penetrate.

Famine has not spread across our land, but there is no barrier against such a calamity. We have not suffered a nuclear disaster of great proportions, but that can happen in a world with lunatics running loose with nuclear know-how. This book is to add variety to the good times we now enjoy. We have the option of exploring kudzu as a food, and are not driven to it as an alternative to starvation.

Netka Greene worked with kudzu in Tennessee for more than 20 years. This is a quote from her journal: "There were times when all I had to give my hungry children was a kudzu root to chew and suck on like sugar cane. It stopped the hunger pains. If times get that hard again, or something goes wrong with that nuclear place over in Oak Ridge, I will grab my tools and head for the nearest kudzu patch."

Acknowledgments

My catalysts for writing *Kudzu Cuisine* are the persons who visited my Web site on the Internet: http://www.kudzukingdom.com, and inquired about kudzu recipes. The mail came from all over the world. I thank each person who wrote. I have collected kudzu recipes for many years but had never given serious thought to sharing them in a book.

Many persons contributed recipes to *Kudzu Cuisine*. Each recipe is printed just as presented, with a proper credit line. Other persons contributed writing about kudzu, and gave me permission to publish. Each writing is printed without editing.

The beautiful photographs of kudzu flowers were made by Jack Anthony of Dahlonega, Georgia. You may view a vast array of stunning photographs of kudzu on his Web site, http://www.stc.net/~janthony/kudzu/kudzu.html.

Last year, I received a personal journal from Netka Greene, who worked with kudzu for more than 20 years. She developed numerous recipes combining various parts of the kudzu vine with ingredients readily available in the South. Netka had, of necessity, fed her family kudzu. After the necessity phase passed, kudzu cuisine became a hobby which she continued to the end of her life. Her work, and the delightful, unpretentious style of writing about it, is a treasure trove! I share her work here as a tribute to her memory.

A special thank-you is due my husband, Jesse Baldwin. He has tolerated kudzu in every form imaginable as I work with it, write about it, and photograph it. Jesse is convinced that kudzu came into his life to test his patience. I am happy to report that he has passed each test, even when he resisted the test mightily!

I acknowledge each contribution with sincere appreciation.

About the Author

My professions are psychologist and writer. My avocations are kudzu and mysteries. Without the benefit of portfolio, I have become a proponent of finding uses for kudzu. In 1996 I coauthored the book *Kudzu The Vine to Love or Hate* with Diane Hoots.

The Nancy Drew mysteries imprinted me for life. In 1998 I coauthored *Unsolved Disappearances in the Great Smoky Mountains*, with Ester Grubb.

This photograph was made in a kudzu patch during a publicity shoot for *Kudzu The Vine to Love or Hate.* Ester Grubb (right in photo) and I were writing *Unsolved Disappearances in the Great Smoky Mountains* at the time. She had never been in a kudzu patch until that day.

Ester and I are currently working on a new mystery. In the spring of 1999 we had a call from a Realtor about an unexplained marker in the boondocks of Sevier County, Tennessee. With cameras in hand, we rushed to the site. This is a photograph of the marker. The inscription is: KESSLER SOME TIMES DEAD IS BETTER. Our goal is to solve the mystery, and write the book during 2000.

Unsolved Disappearances in the Great Smoky Mountains is in many public libraries, sold in bookstores, and on the Internet at http://www.amazon.com, and at all the Visitor Centers in the Great Smoky Mountains National Park.

Kudzu The Vine to Love or Hate, and my other books, are also in libraries, sold in bookstores and by all the major booksellers on the Internet, e.g., Barnes & Noble, Amazon.com, and Borders.

I enjoy hearing from my readers. E-mail is juanittabaldwin@juno.com, or write c/o Suntop Press, PO Box 98, Kodak, Tennessee 37764.

I Met Kudzu One Happy Summer Day

Juanitta Baldwin

While my sister Jane and I were in grammar school, visiting our grandmother in Swain County, North Carolina, was the best part of the summer. A little way "down the branch" was one of the finer houses in her community. The road ran beside the branch, but nobody ever said "down the road." An old lady, whose name I never knew, lived alone in the fine house.

On hot days, kids from the community would invite us to "race in the branch." The race began near Granny's house and ended at the fine house. There was a lot of yelling and splashing. Most days, the old lady would treat us to cold lemonade. We would sit on the porch and tell her all about the race. She always laughed and said the right things.

Across the road from the fine house, the hill was covered in a vine so thick that we could not go through it to get to the woods to pick bright red berries off of little plants with dark green leaves. We called them teaberries because they tasted like teaberry chewing gum.

One day we noticed that the vines on the hill had flowers that smelled like grapes. The old lady explained that it was a special vine called kudzu. The government had planted it to keep the dirt from washing away. We thought kudzu was a funny name, giggled and called each other "Kudzu."

The old lady is gone. Kudzu has crossed the road, arched the branch, and claimed the fine house as its own. The branch we raced and splashed in is now a trickle.

Last summer I climbed to the teaberry patch. Kudzu has claimed most of it, but I found a few beautiful red berries. I went to the fine house, sat on a rock beside the branch, and ate my teaberries. I relived the happy summer day when I met kudzu. For a time, I was a carefree, barefoot kid, thanks to the miracle of memory.

Nutrients in Kudzu

Source: U.S. Department of Agriculture

Nutrients in 100 Grams (3.50 ounces) of Fresh Kudzu (Pueraria Lobata).

Calories 113
Protein 2.1 %
Fiber 20 %
Fat 0.1 %
Calcium 15 Mg.
Phosphorus 18 Mg.
Iron 0.6 Mg.
Chlorophyll and vitamins were present but not measured precisely in this sample.

Nutrients in 100 Grams (3.50 ounces) of Kudzu Powder.

Calories 336
Protein 0.2%
Fat 0.1 %
Carbohydrates 83.1 %
Fiber 0
Ash 0.1 %
Calcium 17 Mg.
Sodium 2 Mg.
Phosphorus 10 Mg.
Iron 2.0 Mg.
Vitamins were present but not measured precisely in this sample.

Nutrients in 100 Grams Dried Kudzu Root.

Protein 13.3%
Fat 2.2%
Sugars 32.1%
Fiber 31.4%
Ash 7.4%
Vitamins were present but not measured precisely in this sample.

Part I
Kudzu Flower Cookery

Photographs by Jack Anthony

Kudzu blooms in late summer, and produces seed pods in autumn. *Pueraria lobata* is the most prevalent variety of kudzu in the United States. Its flowers are variegated shades of magenta and reddish purple. White blossoms are produced by *Pueraria tuberosa*, a variety of kudzu which is much less prevalent. There are other varieties of kudzu, but the culinary uses of these two varieties are the focus of this book.

When kudzu is in bloom, the air is alive with a delightful aroma resembling ripe grapes. The blossoms do not have a grape taste, either fresh or cooked. They have a distinctive, delicate flavor all their own, elusively sweet and refreshing.

Kudzu blossoms appear delicate, but are sturdy. To enjoy a beautiful kudzu bouquet for days, clip kudzu vines hosting the long racemes of wisteria-like flowers. Place the vines in a tall vase filled with water, and out of direct sunlight. A soft fragrance will fill your home.

How to Select and Harvest Kudzu Flowers

Locate a Source of Flowers

Kudzu flowers or blossoms, whichever you prefer to call them, are generally hidden from view under the dense cover of leaves. It is indeed rare that a mature patch of kudzu does not produce flowers, which means a bountiful supply is available for picking. Blooming is affected by the weather and the geographic location, but look for flowers from early summer until late fall.

 If you do not own a kudzu patch, find one that you can ascertain has not been sprayed with herbicides or pesticides, and not subjected to heavy coatings of dust and/or automobile exhaust pollution. Determine who owns the patch and ask permission to harvest.

Most property owners are delighted to have persons harvest kudzu flowers and any other part of their kudzu patch. No one has ever refused to give me permission, and I have met many interesting persons in the process.

Take Your Sense of Humor to the Kudzu Patch

The Church of God owns a magnificent stand of kudzu covering many acres near my home in Tennessee. The church operates a home for children on land adjacent to this kudzu patch, and expends much effort to keep a separation between Church and Kudzu. I asked and received permission to "take all the kudzu you want, and all of it if you can!"

On one kudzu-gathering expedition an acquaintance I had made at the kudzu patch came to where I was picking kudzu flowers.
"Glad to see you," he said, with a broad and very impish grin. "Mind if I make your picture?" He pulled a small one-time-use camera from his shirt pocket.
 "I don't mind, but you must tell me why. You look like you are up to no good!"
Chuckling, he explained. "I want your picture to show my brother. I told him about you getting kudzu, and he said, 'I'll bet you never see her again!' I said you looked to be in good health, and asked him why he thought that.
"He said, 'That woman may be healthy, but if she is cavorting in the kudzu, she must have escaped from the nut house! They have probably found her by now!'"
I exploded with laughter. "How much did you bet? I may demand part of it."
"Oh, we just bet with words to get one up on each other. We've been joshing like that since we were boys."
"Oh well," I replied with mock disappointment, "make the picture."
He snapped the camera, and promised me a picture. "I was sure you would not be offended at what my brother said. He just said all that to be funny. He feeds his cattle kudzu."
"Tell your brother he is funny, but you win the bet."
Several weeks later my acquaintance and his brother came by. The brother would not agree that my acquaintance had won the bet until he made sure the picture was not a fake!

Clothing

Appropriate clothing is an absolute must if you go beyond the fringes of a dense kudzu patch. Wear shoes and socks that are made for rough outdoor terrain. Kudzu cannot abide bare ground. It grows in every pattern imaginable, turning even the most level ground into an obstacle course.

Wear rugged pants, a shirt with long sleeves, and a hat. Take a pair of cotton gloves with you. It is not generally necessary to wear gloves to pick flowers, but they are handy in pulling vines out of the way to get to the flowers. The hat is to protect you from falling debris if you pull vines from over your head. Take an ample supply of drinking water.

Take a bucket, or basket, with a handle that fits comfortably over your arm, to hold the flowers you pick. Plastic bags are not suitable, because they are difficult to open to put the flowers in, and they hold heat, which hastens deterioration.

Remember, We Are Intruders in the Kudzu Patch

Kudzu patches are home to animals and insects. Honeybees and wild bees love kudzu flowers and are quick to defend their turf against intruders. Perhaps it is because they have a mission. Bees are the only insects known to be pollinators of kudzu.

Kudzu honey is rare, but wonderful. These beehives in the photograph below were placed adjacent to the kudzu patch at the right of the picture during blooming time. The owners are checking their harvest. Note that they are dressed properly!

I was fortunate enough to receive a jar of the kudzu honey. It was a light, golden magenta, and very thick.

Our jar of kudzu blossom honey is pictured here before a pancake breakfast next morning! It reminded me of sourwood blossom honey because it has a delightful lingering quality.

Unfortunately, I do not know of a commercial supplier of kudzu honey. The producers I contacted have more regular customers than they have honey.

Other Critters in Kudzu Patches

Frogs, lizards, snakes, groundhogs, spiders, birds, and probably many critters I do not know about establish their habitat in kudzu patches. These residents are not as aggressive as bees, but never forget they are there.

Diane Hoots has harvested kudzu for many years. She suggests making loud noises! It must be effective, she says, because she has never seen a snake or had an unpleasant experience with any critter.

Groundhogs tunnel in the earth. I have encountered only one groundhog. She/he sat upright and watched me for a few moments, chewing something, then scrambled into the narrow tunnel to its home.

I have also encountered bees without incident, except the day I went into the kudzu patch wearing Giorgio! They gave me a buzzing, but I escaped without a sting, and an indelible memory that perfume attracts bees.

Picking Flowers

Buds tend to cling to the stem, but fully opened petals are easy to pull. Some people snip the whole raceme and pick the flowers later; others pick just the flowers.

If you are picking kudzu blossoms, there is no doubt you are in a kudzu patch. But other plants with the three-leaf pattern, *which must be avoided,* grow in and around kudzu patches. Two of the most dangerous to most humans are poison oak and poison ivy.

Kudzu is classified as a wild plant, although many persons cultivate it as human and animal food. Before you eat any wild plant, be sure of its identity. If you are prone to allergies, eat only a small portion of any new food, wild or otherwise, as a test.

Harvesting kudzu blossoms can be great exercise and a satisfying experience, but remember it is not like snipping wisteria in your yard. Don't be afraid. Be smart.

Enjoy Your Kudzu Blossom Bounty

As soon as possible, wash the kudzu blossoms gently, but very thoroughly, in cool water, drain, then store them in sealed containers in the refrigerator. They will remain fresh in prime condition for about twenty-four hours. I have kept them up to three days, but only the most hardy in the lot retained good color and vitality. Kudzu blossoms can be frozen for later use. Spread in a single layer and freeze. Place the frozen blossoms in airtight containers. Another option is to place the blossoms in airtight containers, cover with water and freeze.

Fresh blossoms are delicious as well as decorative. After all your labor in the kudzu patch, you probably need a snack. Spread cream cheese or peanut butter on a couple of your favorite crackers and garnish with fresh kudzu blossoms and tiny kudzu leaves.

Crystallized Kudzu Blossoms

Crystallized kudzu blossoms are a unique, delicious dessert. They are also an elegant finishing touch for cakes and other desserts.

This recipe uses gum arabic and rose water instead of beaten raw egg whites, because of the problems raw eggs can cause. Gum arabic and rose water are sold in cake-decorating supply stores and larger drugstores.

Buy in advance: Gum arabic, rose water, and superfine sugar

Preparation:
Dissolve 3 tablespoons gum arabic in 6 ounces of rose water.
Immerse each kudzu blossom gently in the gum arabic/rose water solution for a few seconds.
Immediately dip the blossom into the superfine sugar.
Place the blossoms on a plate or wire rack and leave them uncovered at normal room temperature until completely dry to the touch.
Blossoms may be kept in an airtight container in your freezer up to a month.

Kudzu Blossom Jelly

Kudzu blossom jelly has a distinctive, quite mild and pleasant taste. Jelly made from fresh blossoms will range from light burgundy to purple in color. If made with frozen blossoms, it will be in the golden color range.

This jelly courtesy Flora Tolar

This jelly courtesy Diane Hoots

For best results, make jelly as many times as necessary, using the quantities in this recipe. Doubling it does not produce good jelly. It makes about six 5-ounce jars of jelly.

Ingredients:
   4 cups fresh kudzu blossoms, washed and well drained
   1 tablespoon fresh lemon juice
   1- 3/4 ounces pectin
   5 cups granulated sugar

Preparation:
   Bring 4 cups of water to a rolling boil
   Stir kudzu blossoms into the boiling water, cook 2 minutes, then remove from heat
   Allow to stand for about 12 hours, then strain to remove the blossoms from the liquid*
   Place the liquid in a pot, add the lemon juice and pectin, and bring to a rolling boil
   Stir in the sugar, and stir constantly until the liquid reaches a second rolling boil
   Boil for 2-3 minutes, remove from heat and skim off the foam
   Pour into sterilized jars and seal with lids that are airtight
   Place the jars on a rack and submerge in a boiling water bath for 5 minutes
   When cool enough to touch, tighten the lids and turn upside down for 2-5 hours

* Note: The liquid may be made and frozen. Thaw and proceed with the recipe.

Kudzu Blossom Spread

Kudzu blossom spread can be made using this kudzu jelly recipe if you do not strain out the blossoms. It will yield a product similar to the commercial all-fruit spreads. Use the liquefy setting on a blender to process the cooked blossoms until very smooth, then follow the jelly preparation steps. This yields seven/eight 5-ounce jars of kudzu blossom spread.

Poet Elaine Cavanaugh on Kudzu

Shortly after the publication of the book *Kudzu The Vine to Love or Hate* in 1996, which I coauthored with Diane Hoots, Elaine Cavanaugh wrote to us. She has given us permission to share her comments on kudzu with you.

"Am halfway through the Kudzu book. I found it at the library. People amaze me! This book is fascinating. The people who fiddle with Kudzu are, I think, more durable than the plant!

We don't have Kudzu here, but I remember when I saw my first 'lake of Kudzu' in Tryon, North Carolina. Never saw anything so beautiful. Since then, I've lived in Kudzu states and gathered Kudzu blossoms.

Best to you,
Elaine"

While searching the Internet in 1999, I chanced upon a poem, *Gathering Kudzu Flowers in August* by Elaine Cavanaugh! I wrote to her immediately and asked permission to publish this poem. She graciously granted permission.

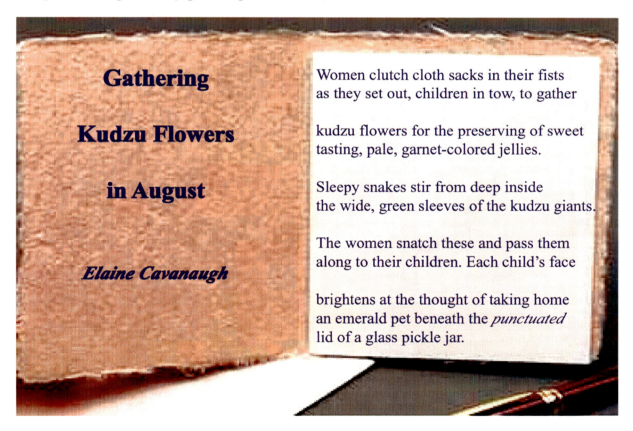

Gathering

Kudzu Flowers

in August

Elaine Cavanaugh

Women clutch cloth sacks in their fists
as they set out, children in tow, to gather

kudzu flowers for the preserving of sweet
tasting, pale, garnet-colored jellies.

Sleepy snakes stir from deep inside
the wide, green sleeves of the kudzu giants.

The women snatch these and pass them
along to their children. Each child's face

brightens at the thought of taking home
an emerald pet beneath the *punctuated*
lid of a glass pickle jar.

Elaine Cavanaugh's poems have appeared in numerous publications, including two chapbooks, *Quiet Rain at Shining Rock* and *Tapestry of Me*. She lives and works in Hartland, Wisconsin. She is a member of the Wisconsin Fellowship of Poets.

Kudzu Blossom Tea

Tea can be made from fresh or dried kudzu blossoms. Experiment to determine how many blossoms produce a cup of tea to your liking. A larger quantity of fresh blossoms than dried blossoms is normally required. Begin with 1/2 cup fresh blossoms, or 1/4 cup of dried blossoms. Pour 2 cups of boiling water over them, and let stand for 3-5 minutes. Strain and enjoy plain, with sugar, cream, lemon or other fruit juice.

Southern States Pasta Salad

Ingredients for 4-5 servings:

    1 pound pasta shells or twirls

    6 strips of bacon, or 6 tablespoons cooking oil

    1/2 cup finely chopped onion

    20 pitted and sliced black or green olives

    1 cup finely chopped celery

    24 fresh kudzu blossoms — chop in half, or smaller if you wish

Preparation:

    Cook pasta to the al dente stage

    Fry the bacon crisp enough to crumble, remove and drain, or heat the oil

    Saute the onion and celery until the onion is clear

    Drain pasta and place in a mixing bowl

    Stir in the onion and celery, olives, kudzu blossoms, and crumble in the bacon

    Serve on a bed of shredded lettuce or other greens

    Garnish with whole fresh or crystallized kudzu blossoms

Kudzu Syrup Recipe from Flora Tolar of Batesville, Mississippi

Flora Tolar has been experimenting with kudzu since 1987. It began one day as she passed by towering vines and smelled the fragrance of the flowers. She researched and found there are no toxins present in kudzu, and that it is a completely edible plant.

After she acquired an arsenal of knowledge about kudzu, and practical experience with it, she began offering seminars. Flora tells all seminar attendees, and the press covering her seminars and other kudzu activities, "I really want people to let go of the notion that Kudzu can't be eaten. I come from a generation where people lived off the lands." More of her work appears in *Kudzu Cuisine*.

This is one of her very easy kudzu recipes. Use 1/2 cup kudzu jelly, melted, and 1 pint of white Karo Syrup. Heat until well blended and refrigerate. Use over pancakes or waffles.

Kudzu Wine

I am printing two recipes for kudzu blossom wine. The first recipe is from Flora Tolar. It is simple, direct, and does not require any extraordinary equipment. She warns that it is an old fashioned method which can fail. But it did not fail in 1997, as evidenced by this bottle of her 1997 wine.

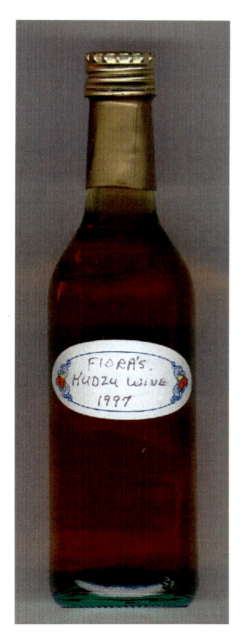

The second recipe, which follows this one, was developed by Netka Greene in 1954. It is in her journal, along with a narrative explaining why she made wine.

Flora's Kudzu Wine Recipe

1/2 gallon of kudzu flowers
4 quarts of water
Cook until flowers lose their color. Strain. Add 2 cups of sugar to liquid. Cover and set overnight. Strain through a cheesecloth. Add 4 cups sugar. Put in cool place and wait for the fermenting to start. Skim daily. On the sixth day I added 2 cups of sugar and bottled on the seventeenth day.

Be sure all the bottles, jars, and corks are sterilized. Fill, leaving air space. Seal and put away for at least six months. It's better after a year.

GOOD LUCK! ENJOY! HAVE FUN! AND MAY GOD BLESS!

In the photgraph at the right is a bottle of Flora's Kudzu Wine Vinegar.

Chicken Soup with Kudzu Sprouts

This is a another of Flora's quick and easy kudzu recipes.

1 can Campbell's Cream of Chicken Soup. Use 3/4 can of water, mix well and bring to a boil. Add 1/2 cup of kudzu sprouts (end of runners). Cook 1 or 2 minutes, stirring often. Serve over toast, rice, or egg noodles.

Kudzu Blossom Wine

This recipe for kudzu blossom wine was created by Netka Greene while living in rural Cocke County, Tennessee. The Greenes were very poor at that time, but that did not stifle Netka's spirit. This is a charming excerpt from her journal explaining why she made wine.

Getting Even with Riley

I learned how to make kudzu blossom wine because I was mad at Riley. He "forgot" to tell me while we were courting that he made moonshine. If my folks back in North Carolina had a hint of this, they would be horrified. Riley knew if he told me we'd never jump over the broomstick. Thank God, he does not drink much of it. "I don't drink my profit," he says.

Papa always kept moonshine and wine, just in case of sickness, he said. Mama made me drink hot water with moonshine and black pepper when I got the measles. Papa and Mama were not sick as often as we younguns smelled it on their breath, but they did not get drunk.

It was not the moonshine itself that rung my chimes. It was the risk old Riley put me at. The law sends moonshiners to jail. I know he did not "forget" to tell me. He did what the preacher calls a sin of omission. Being young and spiteful, I made wine and "plumb forgot" to tell Riley. Ha! Ha! I made wine during the whole 1954 kudzu blooming season, and sold it for cash money, without Riley knowing what I was up to. This is my best wine recipe.

Get these things together before you start:
1 gallon jug
1 big balloon — a little one will not do the job right
2-3 yards of strong twine
4 cups sugar
1 cake Fleischmann's yeast
4-5 quarts of freshly picked kudzu blossoms
Bring in fresh water and put on a kettle full to boil

1. Pick the flowers when they are dry.
2. Wash real good in a dishpan of water with half cup vinegar in it to kill any bugs.
3. Put the blossoms in a canner. Grate the rinds of 1 lemon, 1 grapefruit and 1 orange over them. I have made it with just grapefruit because I did not have any citrus except the grapefruit the welfare gave out, and it worked okay.
4. Pour 2 or 3 quarts of boiling water over the blossoms and stir.
5. Put the lid on the canner and let it stand for 4 full days. The blossoms will float, so stir the mixture twice a day. If you have a good glazed pottery churn, you can put the mixture in it and use the dasher to stir and keep the blossoms from floating. Do not use a wooden churn you churn butter in, or your wine will taste funny.
6. After 4 days have passed, strain the liquid off. Press the blossoms to get all the liquid. You can dry them and put them in cornbread, or feed to your animals.
7. Dissolve the 4 cups of sugar into the liquid.

8. Dissolve 1/2 cake yeast in lukewarm water. Hot water will kill the yeast and your wine won't make. Pour the dissolved yeast into the blossom liquid and stir it good.

9. Pour into your clean gallon jug. Pour enough lukewarm water to fill the jug up to about 3 inches below the neck.

10. Slip the balloon over the top of the neck of the jug. It will flop over, so hold it out of the way and tie it to the neck of the jug with the twine string. Tie it airtight.

11. Put the jug in a cool place like a closet where the temperature is between 60 and 75.

12. If you have done it right, the balloon will swell with gas when your wine is working. Check it about every other day. If the balloon looks like it might pop, untie the twine to let the gas out. Tie it back tight.

13. In about 5 or 6 weeks the balloon will flop over. You have turned water into wine!!!

14. Strain with a good tea towel.

15. Pour the wine back in the jug and screw the top on good. Keep the jug in a cool, dark place like your root cellar or spring house. If you have good bottles with tight tops or corks, you may want to bottle it. Just for the devil of it, I used some of Riley's moonshine bottles.

16. In about 2-3 months, do as Paul the Apostle told Timothy, "Take a little wine for the stomach's sake." The longer you keep wine the better it gets, so I am told.

Riley found out on October 5, 1955, that I was making wine.

We had gone to bed early because Riley had to get up at midnight to do a run at the still. The moon was full and bright. Our two hound dogs were asleep on the porch. We were drifting off to sleep when an ear-splitting shot jerked us wide awake. The dogs set off a howl.

"Damn!" Riley thundered. He jumped up, grabbed his rifle, and ran toward the kitchen door. "Netka, look out the front. If it's the law, I am not here!"

I went out on the porch. It was light as day. I saw nothing but empty fields and the woods beyond. I heard nothing but cowbells and frogs. The dogs lay back down.

"Nothing out here, Riley," I yelled. Then it hit me! Nobody had shot. A bottle of my wine had exploded! I picked up a flashlight and went to the back porch where he was standing, looking everywhere, ready to shoot. "Riley, I think I know what we heard. Come with me to the little room off the back porch."

Riley, still unstrung, held his rifle under his arm as I opened the door. "Good God! This place smells like a still!"

"Yep, looks like a bottle of my wine popped its cork," I said, in what I hope was a real good "I got even with you" voice.

"What wine?" he demanded, in that puffed-up, whiplash tone I hate.

I told him straight out that I just "forgot" to tell him about "wineshining" same as he had "forgot" to tell me about moonshining. I bragged, truthfully, that I had customers waiting for the wine to get done. I finished by asking with offhand satisfaction, "Want to try what's left in this bottle?"

"Zeeeeeee! Right under my nose!" He took a few sips, then made a loud gagging noise. I could see he didn't like the wine, or me making it.

"It will be better in a few weeks." I said, not intending to be bullied. I got my Mason jar, with the cash money in it that I had made selling wine, from its secret hiding place. "See how much money I have made!"

He grinned and hugged me real tight. "Okay! Now we're even!"

Kudzu Flower Fritters

Ingredients:

Mix 1 cup self-rising flour and 1/2 cup self-rising cornmeal
1 egg
1 cup kudzu flowers, minced or finely chopped
3/4 cup buttermilk
1 tablespoon safflower or other cooking oil

Preparation:

Beat the egg in a mixing bowl, add the buttermilk, oil, and flour/cornmeal mixture. Stir until the batter is smooth, then fold in the kudzu flowers. Preheat the griddle to 300 degrees, and spray lightly with cooking spray or coat lightly with cooking oil. Spoon the batter onto the griddle and cook until each fritter is golden brown on each side.

Kudzu Blossom Ice Cream in an Ice Cream Machine

Ingredients:

8 ounces whole milk
3 ounces fresh kudzu blossoms
1 ounce crystallized ginger
1 cup sugar
8 ounces heavy cream
3 eggs

Preparation:

Place the milk, kudzu blossoms, ginger and sugar in a blender and blend until smooth
Pour into a pan on very low heat
Beat the eggs until frothy, and add to the mixture
Cook until you are certain the eggs are well cooked, then remove from heat
Add the cream, stir, and refrigerate until very cold
Following the directions for the ice cream machine you are using, make all or part of the mixture. Freeze any unused mixture. When ready to use, thaw completely, but keep very cold. Stir to dissolve any lumps before pouring into the ice cream freezer.

Kudzu Blossom Syrup

Diane Hoots has been making kudzu blossom syrup since 1990. She says she was making a batch of kudzu blossom jelly that would not thicken as much as required for a good quality jelly.

After fretting a bit, she realized she had a delicious kudzu blossom syrup! From that day on, she has been making syrup. She contracts with a commercial firm to manufacture kudzu blossom jelly and syrup for her company, Krazy Kudzu Products, Ltd.

Kudzu Blossom Vinegar

The English word "vinegar" is a combination of the French *vinaigre* — *vin* for wine and *aigre* for sour. And that is exactly what vinegar is — soured wine. Knowing this, the simplest way to make kudzu blossom vinegar is to expose a bottle of kudzu blossom wine to the open air in the summer sun and allow it to sour. In about two weeks vinegar is created. An alternative is to use this recipe.

Ingredients:
>   2 quarts water
>   2 quarts fresh, washed kudzu blossoms
>   1 pound white raisins, separated to remove any clusters

Preparation:

Place the kudzu blossoms and raisins in a wide-mouth glass jar and pour the water over them. Do not use plastic, iron, or aluminum containers. Cover with a lightweight cloth. Set in a warm place for two months.

Homemade vinegar is not the same as commercially pasteurized vinegar. In its natural state, vinegar is alive with organisms. One common organism is the vinegar fly, of the genus Drosophila. They lay eggs which hatch out into larvae and thrive in vinegar. The flies can be killed by pasteurizing the vinegar after it has fermented completely and has been filtered.

During the two fermentation processes required to make vinegar, a sticky floating lump will form. This is called "mother-of-vinegar." It is formed by the essential bacteria which creates vinegar. After two months have passed, lift it off and discard. All of it must be removed to prevent further fermentation. The certain way to remove the "mother-of-vinegar" is to filter the vinegar after it has fermented. A coffee filter works fine for this.

The vinegar is now ready to be bottled and stored. It will keep almost indefinitely if it is pasteurized. Sterilize the bottles. Heat the vinegar, pour into the bottles, and place in a hot water bath. The *vinegar* must reach at least 140 degrees F, but do not heat over 160 degrees. Use a cooking thermometer to determine that the correct temperature is met. Cap the bottles with sterilized caps as soon as they are sufficiently cooled.

Store the vinegar bottles at room temperature out of direct sunlight. The acid in vinegar acts as a preservative. Color changes may occur after a long period of storage, but this is only an aesthetic change.

Caution: As with any homemade vinegar, kudzu blossom vinegar is good for salad dressing and general cookery, but its acidity may not be high enough to use for pickling or canning. An acidity of at least 4 percent is required for safe pickling or canning.

There are several tests you can do at home to determine the acidity, but they are complicated. Unless you are into vinegar-making big time, and have precise information and skill, it is probably best to buy commercial vinegar for pickling and canning.

This Is Not the Vinegar Bible

The distinction of printing "The Vinegar Bible" belongs to Clarendon Press in Oxford, England. In 1717, Clarendon printed a new edition of the Holy Bible. The typesetter placed the word "vinegar" where "vineyard" should have been in the top-of-the-page running head of the 22nd chapter of the book of Luke. The error was discovered in a short time, and the edition became known as "The Vinegar Bible." It is the name by which Clarendon's 1717 edition of the Bible is known today.

Kudzu Blossom Vinegar Cookies

Vinegar's unique flavoring qualities perk up food, often changing it from ordinary to gourmet. These cookies are a prime example. They have a sweet and sour taste. The vinegar taste is subdued, but the cookies would not be the same without it.

Ingredients:
    1 1/4 cups self-rising flour
    4 ounces salted butter; margarine will not produce a good cookie
    3 tablespoons kudzu blossom vinegar
    1 egg
    2/3 cup raisins

Preparation:
    Let the butter soften to room temperature before you begin. Preheat the oven to 325 degrees. Beat the egg slightly, stir in the butter, vinegar, flour and raisins. Spoon on to pre-heated cookie sheet and bake until a light, golden brown, between 10-11 minutes in an electric stove. This recipe works with any good vinegar.

Splash Kudzu Blossom Vinegar for Robust Flavor without Salt

Splash your kudzu blossom vinegar on raw cucumbers, lettuce, carrots and cabbage before adding them to a salad, or serve with the vinegar only. An added bonus is that the acid in it helps digest cellulose. Use kudzu blossom vinegar in your favorite salad dressing recipe.

Could Cleopatra have Won her Wager with Kudzu Blossom Vinegar?

Cleopatra, the famed queen of Egypt, loved to confound her guests with wagers, so history records. On one occasion she made a wager that she could consume the value of a million sesterces in a single meal. Most guests thought this impossible, and bet against her.

She asked her guests to watch as she dropped a million sesterces worth of pearls into a glass of vinegar. At the end of the meal, she drank the dissolved pearls! Cleopatra knew vinegar was a good solvent, but odds are it was not kudzu blossom vinegar!

Netka Greene's Very Fine Syllabub

This is an excerpt from Netka's journal:

It has been 15 years since I first made wine. Times were hard then, so I used kudzu flowers. As times got better, I had apples and cherries to use. But I still love the taste of kudzu blossom wine. I use it in a recipe I got when Riley and I took a bus trip to Williamsburg, Virginia.

At one of the nice places they had the menu posted outside. We read it, but the prices were beyond our means. They wrote a lot about was their "Very Fine Syllabub," and they told what was in it. I wrote that down when we got back on the tour bus. I made it at Christmas and again at Easter. It is easy to do and good to serve to anybody but the teetotalers.

1 quart heavy cream
1 pound superfine sugar
3 lemons
1 pint kudzu blossom wine — I have made it with others and it works okay

Mix the cream and sugar. Grate the rind from the lemons into the mixture. Squeeze the juice in too. Pour in the wine and beat it all. The place in Williamsburg said to beat it for half an hour, I guess by hand. I put it in the mixer at low speed and do something else for about 15 minutes. Serve in about 3 days for the best flavor. It will keep longer but is not as good.

One of my wine customers from the old days came by at Christmas, and enjoyed one of my very fine syllabubs. Riley told him about how he found out I was "wineshining!" He laughed and said that served a bootlegger right. He said that some of my kudzu wine he bought was so bitter that he had put it up and forgot it for years. When he found it, he started to throw it out but tasted it first. "Never got throwed out," he said. "It was real good."

Curried Carrots with Kudzu Blossoms

Ingredients for 4 Servings:
1 pound baby carrots, peeled, and cooked until tender
1/2 cup raisins
1/2 cup fresh kudzu blossoms, washed and drained
1-1/2 teaspoons sugar or honey
2 teaspoons prepared mustard
1/2 teaspoon curry powder
1 tablespoon lemon juice.

Preparation:
Combine the carrots, raisins, kudzu blossoms, and 3 tablespoons of water. Heat and stir until the raisins puff. Mix, then add remaining ingredients. Cook over low heat 2-3 minutes, stirring constantly to prevent scorching. It is done when the carrots are glazed.

Dire Prediction for Flora Tolar

Flora Tolar recalls, "Seems strange, when I first developed some of my kudzu products folks said, 'You are crazy. That stuff will kill you!' "

That dire prediction has not come true. With the arrival of the millennium, Flora is still very much alive and working with kudzu. Has she given any thought to stopping? "Yes, but I can't, I'm too tangled in the stuff!" A poem she wrote some years ago explains it all.

It Was Just Kudzu and Me

My love affair with Kudzu didn't happen overnight, it grew on me.
We didn't try to hide under the lush foliage
or become entangled, but I knew it was meant to be.
It was just Kudzu and me.

I knew I could never control it, but I could manipulate it.
I could twine it around my whole being or give it
room to roam a bit, but this I knew,
it was just Kudzu and me.

First came the Kudzu Jelly. Oh! How sweet.
Then came the Kudzu Fudge — you be the judge.
Next came the Kudzu Wine — my that's fine.
It was just Kudzu and me.

But it didn't stop there — the Kudzu Family grew.
Kudzu Stir Fry came forth with a cry,
with just the right spices, give it a try.
It was just Kudzu and me.

We'd gone too far to turn back.
Kudzu salve made its debut with Kudzu Tincture,
not the last of my adventure.
It was just Kudzu and me.

The years have been good, we're still entwined.
Ready to settle down with a cup of Kudzu Tea, to unwind
for as you can see,
it's just Kudzu and me.

Part II
Kudzu Leaf and Vine Cookery

This is a very tender kudzu vine, with newly formed leaves and young, developing leaves. This size is the best for kudzu leaf and vine cookery. Some persons call new growth at the ends of vines "runners," and the ends of the runners "sprouts" or "shoots."

Flora Tolar gives this advice: "Use only tender leaves and sprouts of the kudzu plant. Otherwise the leaves will be a tough as a barnyard rooster!"

Kudzu Snack Chips — Deep Fried Leaves
Edith Edwards

Gather clean, young 3-inch leaves in the cooler evenings of summer. Place in Ziploc bag in refrigerator. Several hours before you wish to eat them, make a tempura batter for coating the leaves prior to frying. This is Edith's original Cornmeal Tempura Batter recipe.

1/2 cup plain flour
1/2 cup plain cornmeal
2 tablespoons kudzu powder (dissolved in 1/4 cup cold water)
1 teaspoon baking powder
1/2 teaspoon salt
2 egg whites (lightly beaten)
3/4 cup cold water
Combine dry ingredients, add egg whites and water. Stir well, chill.

1) I use a narrow cooker, like a "Fry-Daddy Jr." Pour oil in container to line suggested, and heat to 375 degrees. Have ready a slotted spoon, to lift chips out of hot oil and lay on paper toweling to absorb dripping after frying.

2) Place 2 bowls on counter, 1 of iced water and 1 of tempura batter (stir batter). Now you are ready to take chilled green kudzu leaves out of refrigerator.

3) Dip 1 leaf into iced water, let it drain off, then put it into tempura batter, drain a little, then put in hot oil. Careful, it will splatter!

4) Cook about 10 to 15 seconds till nicely browned, and turn over with spoon, let cook about 10 more seconds, remove from oil and drain on paper towel. Presto...Kudzu Snack Chips! High in protein and fiber, and a real nice appetizer. You can dip in a sauce, sprinkle parmesan cheese on, or eat as is.

One secret to delicious and crisp chips is the chilled batter and the chilled leaves. The use of kudzu powder is the other secret to creating light, crisp, and delicate deep-fried foods.

Edith and Henry Edwards Have a Message about Kudzu

The Edwardses' message about kudzu is: Kudzu is a wonderful food source for humans and animals. They practice good kudzu management on their farm, Kudzu Konnection, in Rutherfordton, North Carolina. They also spread the message by radio and television appearances, media interviews, and stories in books and magazines.

Edith fried kudzu leaves at the World's Fair in Knoxville, Tennessee, in 1982. She conducts seminars for garden clubs, church groups, and at Isothermal Community College. They know the speaker has arrived when they see an automobile sporting a license plate: KUDZU!

Edith vividly remembers the date she first cooked and ate kudzu — August 22, 1981. The Edwardses had moved to Henry's ancestral home in 1961, and established a Holstein dairy operation. They relied on kudzu as the main source of feed for their cattle and other animals, but it had not occurred to them that it was a valuable human food. The revelation came when Edith read *The Book of Kudzu* by Williams Shurtleff and Akiko Aoyagi, husband-and-wife writers. She says she had purchased the book several months before she opened it, but once opened, it has stayed open!

Special Spring Meal
Andrea Whitfield McCormick

Kudzu, daffodils, and onion tops are the first things we see on our farm as the snow melts. For several years I have prepared a special spring meal using my original recipes for Pasta Primavera and Spring Cake, to celebrate the coming of spring. It is my favorite season.

Spring Cake

Ingredients:

    1 package prepared white cake mix
    1 cup kudzu leaves, washed, drained and chopped
    1 container of prepared yellow cake icing

Preparation:

Mix the kudzu with whatever liquid is used in the recipe and whirl in a blender until the mixture is smooth and green. If an egg is used, add to the mixture and whirl for a few seconds. Add the mixture to the dry cake mix and bake as directed on the package. The batter will be a lovely shade of spring green. Ice the cake and decorate with a fresh kudzu leaf.

Pasta Primavera

Ingredients for 6 Servings:

10 ounces colored pasta
1 cup tender kudzu vines — no leaves
8-10 green onions — use the whole onion
2 medium size carrots
1 large red sweet pepper
2 stalks celery
1/2 cup pecans — I like to use the halves
2 tablespoons vinegar
1 15-ounce can of peeled, diced tomatoes

Preparation:

While the pasta is cooking to al dente, snip the kudzu vines and green onions into 1/2-inch lengths. Cut the carrots, celery, and pepper into thin 1-inch sticks. In a wok or skillet, use a bit of oil to stir-fry the vegetables and pecans until crisp tender. Add the vinegar, then tomatoes, and bring to a boil. Drain the pasta, and mix it with the vegetable mixture. Serve immediately. I always pick a bunch of daffodils for the table.

Preparation for Use and Storage of Fresh Kudzu

Wash kudzu very thoroughly in cold water to remove dirt and insects. Many persons recommend soaking 10 to 20 minutes in salt water. Rinse and drain. If the kudzu is to be used within an hour, leave at room temperature. If not, place in an airtight container or plastic bag and refrigerate. Kudzu will keep several days. The key to keeping kudzu, or other greens, in good condition is to store them with a paper towel. Any moisture still clinging to the kudzu will drip onto the towel, and create enough humidity to keep it from drying out.

As you will note in the photographs of kudzu vines and leaves in *Kudzu Cuisine,* they are covered with a soft fuzz. The fuzz wilts when the kudzu is cooked, but is noticeable when it is used raw. Most of the persons I spoke with who use fresh kudzu do not mind the fuzz, but I do not like it. It can't be removed, so when using uncooked kudzu, I dip it in boiling water, and immediately plunge it into cold water. It wilts the fuzz. The appearance is changed but not the taste.

Mixing Kudzu with Other Greens

Kudzu complements other cooked greens by adding texture and flavor. It blends nicely with turnip, mustard, and spinach. Use your favorite recipes, and add kudzu.

Turnip, Mustard and Kudzu

2 cups chopped mustard leaves, washed and drained
2 cups chopped kudzu leaves and stems, washed and drained
3 slices stripped lean pork or bacon
1/3 cup vinegar
Salt optional

Mix the greens and place in a boiling pot. Cover with water, add the vinegar and cook until the water is a greenish tan color. Drain. Saute the pork or bacon in the boiling pot. Put the greens back in the pot and add enough water to provide steam. Cover and cook until as tender as you like greens to be.

A variation is to cook the greens until tender, then drain. Dice and saute an onion in with the meat. Pour the greens into the meat/onion mixture, and stir until thoroughly mixed. Cover and cook to the desired doneness.

Another variation on cooking the greens is to saute in butter, or serve with butter.

Fill your cruet with vinegar; many persons like it with greens.

Quick Cook Kudzu and Spinach

1 pound spinach, washed and drained
1 pound tender kudzu leaves, washed and drained
2 tablespoons cooking oil
1/2 teaspoon salt
1 tablespoon butter

Mix the spinach and kudzu.

Use a heavy, deep pot with a lid. Spoon the cooking oil into the pot and heat until the oil is very hot.

Pour the greens into the hot oil, and stir to turn the greens. Continue until all the greens are wilted. Add the salt and butter. Lower the heat to simmer, cover and cook for 5 minutes. Remove the lid and turn the heat to high. There will be liquid in the bottom of the pot. Stir until it is almost gone. Remove from heat, cover until ready to serve. Cut lemon slices for those who may enjoy this dressing.

Kudzu and Pokeweed

Netka Greene cooked wild pokeweed and kudzu to feed her family, because money for food was very hard to come by at times. She called it poke salad, as most Southerners do. Poke is edible only in the early spring, so Netka cooked it with kudzu and canned it. This is what she wrote:

"There is snow on the ground, but tonight we had greens. I opened a can of poke and kudzu greens, put a little pork lard in them and cooked them. They tasted like warmed-over greens. We had cornbread and onions we had raised and dried. The cow is dry. We watch every day hoping she will calf, and give enough milk for it and for us."

Honey Mustard Kudzu Vines with Carrots

Ingredients for 4 Servings:
1-1/2 cups tender kudzu vines cut into 3/4-inch lengths
1/2 cup carrots, cut into thin, 3/4-inch lengths
2 tablespoons honey
2 tablespoons Dijon mustard
1/2 teaspoon dill weed
For a sweeter dish, add 1/4 cup chopped raisins

Preparation:
Steam the carrots about 5 minutes, add the kudzu vines and steam until both are tender crisp. Combine the honey, mustard and dill. Stir into a smooth sauce. Pour the sauce over the hot kudzu vines and carrots. Stir gently until all the vegetables are coated. Allow to stand for 10 minutes over gentle heat before serving.

Rice and Kudzu Quiche
Printed from *101+ Uses For Kudzu*, ISBN 1880308-14-2
by Diane and Matthew Hoots

Ingredients:
- 4 whole eggs
- 2 cups cooked rice
- 1/2 cup finely grated Swiss cheese
- 20-30 fresh young kudzu leaves
- 2 tablespoons butter or margarine
- 1/2 teaspoon salt
- 1 cup cottage cheese
- 1/4 cup grated Parmesan cheese
- 6 tablespoons heavy cream or evaporated milk
- 1/4 teaspoon nutmeg
- 6 drops hot sauce

Preparation and Cooking Instructions:
Preheat oven to 350 degrees
Grease a 9-inch pie pan or use an 9-inch-square cake pan
In a medium bowl beat 1 egg. Add rice and Swiss cheese. Stir well.
Spread mixture evenly in prepared pan, making a crust
Refrigerate until ready to fill and bake
Cook kudzu leaves in small amount of water until tender. Press to remove moisture and chop very fine.
Add butter and set aside.
In a medium bowl beat remaining 3 eggs. Stir in salt, cottage cheese, Parmesan cheese, heavy cream, hot sauce and nutmeg. When blended, stir in kudzu.
Pour into prepared rice crust.
Bake for 30-35 minutes or until firm.

Diane and Matthew Hoots Make Kudzu Their Business

Diane Hoots is a certified science teacher. In 1985, she and her son Matt, then age 9, took a kudzu wreath course at the Anniston Museum of Natural History, Anniston, Alabama. From that time on, kudzu has grown across their lives much as it grows across a field. Diane studied the vine and learned to weave baskets and cook with it. She began teaching kudzu art and craft classes for groups from grammar school age to senior citizen.

What has started as a hobby developed in 1994 into Krazy Kudzu Products, Ltd., a company that markets kudzu products. Matt worked with kudzu all through school and during his service with the U.S. Marine Band in New Orleans, Louisiana. He used kudzu to make jazz figures and sold them at galleries in uptown New Orleans and in historic Algiers Point. Matt is now a college student, and works part time with Diane in Krazy Kudzu, Ltd. He is in the process of developing a Web site to expand their marketing capabilities.

Diane's activities with kudzu have been widely reported in newspapers, on television, and in magazines.

In 1996, Diane was making a presentation at the Family Motor Home Coach National Rally in Perry, Georgia. My husband and I were in the class of several hundred. The large crowd made it impossible to speak with Diane that day. After I returned home I contacted her to tell her I was writing a book on kudzu and asked if I could include an article about her. "Yes," she replied without hesitation, "but only if I can work with you on the book."

After a couple of lengthy telephone calls, I decided to save much of what I had written for another book, and work with Diane on a book. We worked on the book via telephone, mail and fax. During this time, I dubbed Diane "The Kudzu Guru," a title that is well deserved and has stuck. Our book was published in late 1996 under the title *Kudzu The Vine to Love or Hate*. Diane and I met about a year later.

Diane hopes to build a kudzu museum, and weave the world's largest basket. Knowing the Guru as I now do, unless providentially hindered, she will build it!

Kudzu Kandy

This recipe is printed from *101+ Uses For Kudzu* with permission from Diane and Matthew Hoots.

Ingredients:
> 6-8 ounces white chocolate
> 1/4 cup toasted sliced almonds, chopped walnuts, or pecans, or dried fruits
> 1/4 cup baby kudzu leaves

Preparation:
Remove stems from tender baby kudzu leaves. Wash leaves, towel dry, and chop into small pieces. Spread in baking pan in 350-degree preheated oven and "toast" for about 2-5 minutes until leaves are dry. If you wish to use a microwave to dry the kudzu, follow the instructions in the manual for your microwave.

Remove and let cool. Keep away from drafts, because the tiny kudzu pieces are feather-weights and will blow away!

Place broken chocolate in a microwave-safe container and melt at medium heat for 3-5 minutes. Watch to be sure it does not burn. When completely melted, stir in the almonds, or other ingredient you have selected, then gently fold in the toasted kudzu leaves.

Pour immediately into a pan and let cool completely.

Remove the Kudzu Kandy from the pan and break into small chunks, then nibble away!

Warning: This recipe will not make enough to satisfy!!

From the kitchen of Merridum
The Inn at Merridum
Union, South Carolina 29379
Telephone (803) 427-7052

Flora Tolar's Oriental Kudzu Stir Fry

In a skillet add: 2 tablespoons olive oil, 3 minced garlic cloves. Cook until light brown.

Add about a quart of kudzu leaves, 1 can of Swanson's Oriental Broth, and 1 or 2 teaspoons Kikkoman Soy Sauce (more or less to your taste). Stir until leaves begin to wilt.

Add 1 can of slivered water chestnuts. Stir. Cover and steam 4 to 5 minutes or until the kudzu is tender; stir often.

Serve over rice or noodles.

Cooked Vegetable/Kudzu Salad

This recipe moves salad beyond the plate of iceberg lettuce and cardboard tomatoes. Be daring and serve it to your Doubting Thomas friends. It is quick and can be made ahead.

Ingredients for Salad:
  1 cup of carrots, cut into 1-inch lengths. Use very small carrots if they are available. If not, peel the large carrots and slice them thinly. Cook until crisp tender.
  1 cup of cooked baby lima beans, fresh or frozen
  1 cup whole cooked kernel corn, fresh, canned or frozen
  1 cup of tender kudzu vines, cut into 1/2 lengths, cooked or steamed to crisp tender
Ingredients for Dressing:
  1/2 cup sour cream
  1/2 cup mayonnaise
  1 tablespoon mild prepared mustard or 1 tablespoon of vinegar
  1 tablespoon sugar
Ingredients for Garnish:
  1 cup of cooked beets, cut into shoestrings
  1 pound of cream cheese, cut into long strips. To cut the cream cheese smoothly, place the knife blade inside a piece of paper that is used to wrap butter, with the side of the paper that has been next to the butter on the outside so it will touch the cheese.
  Tiny kudzu leaves and your favorite type of lettuce leaves, to line the plate or bowl
Preparation:
  Mix the cooked vegetables, except the beets, and chill thoroughly.
  Mix the ingredients for the dressing. Season to taste with salt, garlic salt, or ground white pepper. Pour over the chilled vegetables and mix until all the vegetables are coated.
  Line a large plate or bowl with the kudzu and lettuce leaves, alternating to create a beautiful interlaced pattern.
  Pile the dressed vegetables on the leaves and garnish the entire top with the shoestring beets and strips of cream cheese. A very pretty pattern can be made quickly by placing a small quantity of the red beets and topping with the white cheese.
Substitution: A prepared cream dressing may be used.

Fresh Vegetable Salad with Fuzzless Kudzu

This salad is a medley of greens, sliced canned mushrooms, fresh sliced cucumbers and cherry tomatoes. Kudzu leaves and tiny stems which have been dipped in boiling water to wilt the fuzz are mixed with endive, spinach, and escarole.

Dress with Italian or honey-mustard dressing. This salad can be served as a main dish by adding protein such as cooked garbanzos, diced chicken or tuna.

Rolled Beef and Kudzu Loaf
Tony DeAnniaro

Ingredients:

1 envelope of prepared onion soup mix
2 pounds ground beef
1 cup cooked, minced kudzu leaves and stems
2 large eggs
1 16-ounce can of peeled and diced tomatoes, seasoned with pepper and onion
1-1/2 cups fresh bread crumbs
1 teaspoon salt
1 teaspoon black pepper
1 teaspoon sugar
1/2 pound grated Parmesan cheese
3/4 cup water or V-8 juice

Preparation:

Preheat oven to 350 degrees

In a large bowl combine all the ingredients except the cheese and tomatoes, and stir until very well mixed. The mixture should be very thick.

Pour the mixture on wax paper, or a nonstick surface. Flatten the mixture into a rectangle shape about 3/4 inch thick.

Sprinkle the rectangle with a light coating of Parmesan cheese.

Now roll the rectangle lengthwise as you would roll a jelly roll. When rolled, press the end closed to seal in the cheese.

Place in a baking pan, sealed side down.

Bake uncovered 30 minutes.

Remove from oven and pour tomatoes over the loaf.

Return to oven and bake 30 minutes, still uncovered.

Let stand 10 minutes before serving.

Variation:

Use a prepared dressing mix in lieu of fresh bread crumbs, and add more liquid.

Chow Chow with Kudzu
Netka Greene

Ingredients for 4 Pints:

    1 quart finely chopped cabbage
    3 cups green tomatoes, chopped into cubes about 3/4-inch diameter
    1 cup minced kudzu vines and leaves
    1 cup red bell pepper
    1 cup yellow bell pepper
    1/2 cup hot green pepper, minced
    2 teaspoons celery seeds
    2 teaspoons mustard seeds — and 1 teaspoon dry mustard if you want tart chow chow
    1 cup granulated sugar
    1/2 cup minced onion
    2 cups white vinegar

Preparation:

Put all the vegetables in a big dishpan and sprinkle with a lot of salt. Cover and let stand 8 hours in a cool place to let the salt draw out the water.

Just before the 8 hours are up, make the spice mixture. Pour the vinegar into a pot big enough to hold the chow chow vegetables. You can use your enamel canner, but don't use a metal pot or your chow chow will taste funny. Put the spices in the vinegar, and simmer for 20 minutes. Sterilize 5 pint jars. This recipe makes 4, but one might break.

Strain the vegetables through a sterilized rag to remove all the liquid that has accumulated. Pour into spice mixture and bring to a rolling boil and cook for 1 or 2 minutes. While boiling hot, fill sterilized jars, leaving an inch for expansion space. Cap the jars with sterilized lids. When cool enough, tighten the lids and turn upside down to seal. When fully cooled, turn up and tighten the lids.

Note: The woman from the farm office said to put the jars in a hot water bath. I don't do this, because my jars are sterilized, and so are my utensils. So don't forget to sterilize your funnel, spoons and cups you use to put what you are canning into the jars.

Corn and Kudzu Cornsticks

Ingredients for 12 Cornsticks:

    2 cups cornmeal mix
    3/4 cup yellow cream-style corn
    3/4 cup minced, very young kudzu vines
    1 egg
    1 tablespoon hot red pepper, minced very fine
    Buttermilk, if required to thin

Preparation:

Place the cornmeal in a bowl with the kudzu and pepper, mix. Add the corn and egg and stir well. Use buttermilk to thin if mixture is too stiff. Spray or oil a corn stick pan and preheat it. Fill pan and bake in preheated 450-degree oven 15 minutes or until golden brown.

27

Part III
Kudzu Root Cookery

Kudzu Powder

Kudzu powder is a high-quality starch extracted from huge kudzu roots which grow deep in the earth. It is the most widely used form in which kudzu roots are used in cooking. Starch-bearing roots average 7-10 feet in length and weigh hundreds of pounds. The labor required to dig the roots and extract the starch makes kudzu powder very expensive.

This is a photograph of a big kudzu root, but not a good source for starch. Only seedlings produce tap roots, from which starch can be extracted in quantity.

Photograph courtesy Flora Tolar

All the kudzu powder sold commercially in the United States is imported from Korea and Japan. It is sold commercially under the names "Kudzu Powder," "Kudzu Root Powder," " Kudzu Root Starch," "Kudzu Starch," and "Kudzu Flour." Consumers should be aware that few of these products are pure kudzu starch. Kudzu starch is mixed with other starches, such as potato starch, but laws in Korea and Japan do not require precise labeling.

Pure kudzu starch usually comes in a chunk form which must be broken into pieces, dissolved in water, or powdered, prior to use. It is almost always labeled as 100% pure kudzu starch, and is much more expensive than the mixed powders. When pure kudzu powder is dissolved in water, and heated, it becomes almost transparent. Mixed powders are in the golden color range and are translucent.

These are pictures of kudzu powder which I purchased from a local health food store. Although I was assured it was "pure kudzu starch in powder form," it was not. However, it did have enough kudzu starch in it to be superior to arrowroot or similar starches.

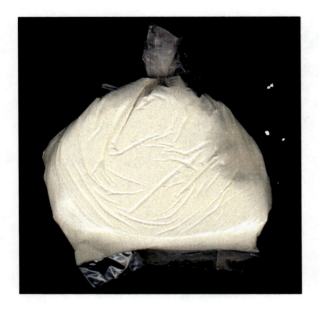 

Kudzu powder is a superb thickening, jelling and glazing starch. Its transparent/translucent quality adds sheen to sauces and jelled desserts. Although kudzu powder has a unique taste and aroma, it blends with other ingredients, and does not leave a starchy taste or texture. Jelled dishes made with kudzu powder hold their firmness at room temperature.

These are photographs of kudzu powder which demonstrate its thickening quality. The sauce base in the measuring spoon was made with 1 tablespoon of kudzu powder cooked in one cup of water. The color changed to the golden hue while being heated.

There are 3 tablespoons of uncooked kudzu powder mixed with about an equal amount of water in the bowl. It turned caramel color before it was mixed with other ingredients and cooked to make caramel fudge. The fudge was wonderful!

Chemically, kudzu powder is alkaline. If used in a dish with acidic liquids, such as lemon juice, more kudzu powder is required than in recipes using water or other alkaline liquids. This is an equivalent guide for kudzu powder:

3/4 teaspoon kudzu powder = 3 teaspoons wheat flour
1-1/2 teaspoons kudzu powder = 1 tablespoon arrowroot
4-1/2 teaspoons kudzu powder = 1 tablespoon cornstarch

Kudzu-Mochi

On one of my frequent Internet searches, I chanced upon a beautiful photograph of a Japanese confection called kudzu-mochi at http://www.kitchoan.com. One box cost $11.00, plus shipping. I yielded to temptation and ordered a box. The caption stated, "The genuine kudzu starch used in these kudzu-mochi cakes is what enhances the taste." The cakes looked tiny, and when the box arrived there were four confections, each 2 by 2 1/2 inches. The taste was as delicious as promised. I located several kudzu-mochi recipes, selected the ingredients from each recipe I like best, and made them. Not quite the same, but not as expensive!

Ingredients:
3/4 cup pasteurized apple juice
1/3 cup kudzu powder
4 tablespoons bread flour
6 tablespoons corn syrup — 3 in mixture, 3 for coating the cakes
1/4 teaspoon salt

Preparation:
Place all the ingredients, except 3 tablespoons of syrup, in a blender and blend until very smooth. Pour into a shallow saucepan and place on medium heat. Stir constantly until the mixture boils and begins to thicken. Reduce the heat to low, and stir until the mixture becomes very thick. Remove from heat, pour onto a cool plate that has been sprayed with a bit of cooking spray. Cool to room temperature.

Cut into squares and place far enough apart to reach to coat all the surfaces. Heat the remaining 3 tablespoons of syrup. Use a pastry brush to lightly coat each kudzu-mochi cake.

Pineapple Kudzu Pie

Ingredients:
1 16-ounce can sweetened crushed pineapple
3-1/2 tablespoons kudzu powder
1 prepared pie shell
1 16-ounce jar marshmallow cream

Preparation:
Preheat oven to 300 degrees.

Combine the crushed pineapple and kudzu powder and stir until smooth. Pour into prepared pie shell. Bake on middle rack 30 minutes or until

the top is light brown and firm to the touch. Remove from oven and let cool at room temperature. When cool to the touch, decorate with the marshmallow cream, and place in freezer until the marshmallow cream is very firm so it will not melt while being browned.

Turn oven to broiler setting. If the oven is electrical, allow all the broiler coils to reach the glowing stage. Place the pie on the top rack and brown. This usually take about 3 minutes, but the time may vary from oven to oven, so watch to be sure the pie does not burn.

Treats for Travel — or Anywhere, Any Time

Ingredients:
- 1 pound pecans
- 1 pound raisins
- 1 pound dried bananas
- 1 cup apple juice or apple cider
- 1 tablespoon kudzu powder

Preparation:

Dissolve the kudzu powder in the juice or cider and heat, stirring until it clears. Mix the pecans, raisins and bananas. Pour liquid over the mixture and mix. Shape into balls.

Skillet Cabbage with Kudzu
Jill Waterside

Cabbage has been burned at the stake! By this, I mean that cabbage has been overcooked by so many persons for so many years that it has gained an undeserved reputation as a smelly, sharp vegetable. Not so, if cooking is stopped when cabbage reaches the tender stage. I have used this recipe for years. One day innovation struck, and I added minced kudzu and sweet red pepper. The eye appeal was like turning on a neon light on a street at dusk!

Ingredients for 4 Servings:
- 6 cups coarsely ground cabbage
- 2 tablespoons vinegar
- 1 cup minced kudzu leaves
- 1 cup diced sweet red pepper
- 3 tablespoons honey
- 1-1/2 teaspoons prepared mustard
- 1/2 cup sour cream
- 1 teaspoon kudzu powder, dissolved in 2 tablespoons water

Preparation:

Bring 1/4 cup water to a boil in a large skillet. Stir in the cabbage/kudzu. Reduce heat to low, cover, and cook for 6 minutes. Add the pepper and kudzu powder. Stir briskly until there is a sheen on the cabbage/kudzu. Mix the honey with the other ingredients, and stir into the cabbage/kudzu. Cook uncovered until the cabbage is tender but crunchy. Serve immediately.

Kudzu Noodles

In Japan, dry kudzu noodles are sold in highly decorated packages in supermarkets. These noodles resemble very thin spaghetti. The "real kudzu" noodles are made with 100 percent kudzu powder. As with kudzu powder, manufacturers of kudzu noodles add other starches, but under Japanese law they do not have to label the contents to alert the consumer. In some instances, kudzu noodles contain no kudzu powder at all.

Kudzu noodles are available in a few health food stores in the United States. If you wish to purchase them, look for a package which states the contents. Cooking directions and serving suggestions are printed on most packages.

Fresh Vegetable Soup with Kousin Kudzu
Armond and Kathy Millstone, Swain County, North Carolina

We know that kudzu is a legume, a huggin' cousin to the beans and peas we like so much. We garden near a thick stand of kudzu. One day Kathy wondered aloud what kudzu tasted like. She bit a vine and rendered a verdict: "Not bad."

I laughed, then had second thoughts. "It is a waste to pull all this stuff out and throw it away. Why don't we try and make something edible out of it?" Kathy said she'd go to the library and see if she could find out how to cook it. She did, and we now eat lots of kudzu, and so do our friends. Some we've told. Some we may never tell, especially the one who went to the Swain County Workshop on killing kudzu! If any of them read your book, we may have to "fess up!"

Ingredients:
Chop all the vegetables to the size you like in your soup. We aim for 1/2 inch.
3 strips bacon — fry it first, remove, then crumble it over the soup when it is served
16 ounces of fresh or canned tomatoes, peeled and diced
1 cup celery
1 cup carrots
1 cup green peas
1 cup green beans
1 cup Irish potato
1 cup onion, chopped
1 cup kudzu vines and leaves, chopped
1 cup water or liquid saved from cooking other vegetables — adjust liquid as necessary
2 tablespoons kudzu root powder

Preparation:
Fry the bacon in a heavy soup pot, then remove. Fry the potato, celery and carrots in the bacon fat until they begin to clear Add everything except the kudzu root powder, and bring to boil. Simmer 3 hours on low heat. Dissolve the kudzu powder in 1/4 cup water and stir into the soup to thicken it. Add a bit of sugar and salt. Keeps well, if there is any to keep!

A Description of Kudzu Roots

I am amazed at how many articles state, without any qualification or explanation, that kudzu roots can be dug, cut into cubes, steamed or boiled, and eaten like potatoes. This is a kudzu root which was growing about a foot in the ground. It had vines 20 feet long.

I have cut a section of the root pictured on page 32 to show how woody it is. No cutting this into cubes! Not all roots are this woody, but don't expect to find any roots growing near the top of the ground to have an interior the texture of a potato. Perhaps roots from "way down deep" are different, but I have yet to find anyone who has actually found a root that could be treated as a potato.

The kudzu root pictured on page 32 took root from a node on a kudzu vine which made contact with the soil and had sufficient moisture. While this root has some starch, only roots which begin as seedlings produce tap roots from which a large quantity of starch can be extracted and made into kudzu powder.

Kudzu has served as a famine food in Japan. They probably sucked the juice and chewed raw roots, and hopefully in late fall or winter when the roots are the richest in starch.

Dried Mature Kudzu Root

In the photograph to the left, are slices of dried, mature kudzu root, used to make tea. They can be purchased from health food stores and herbal dealers. The texture is too woody for you to eat with comfort.

This is a primary ingredient in many medicinal teas used in China and Japan.

Tender Kudzu Root Tea

Kudzu roots expand each year. Young tender roots have a mild taste resembling peppermint. They can be cut from the old part of the root and used to brew a refreshing tea. Snip! Steep! Sip! Be sure to brew an extra cup to make Kudzu Root Divine. The recipe is on the next page.

Kudzu Root Divine

Ingredients:
   2 whole eggs, warmed to room temperature
   2 egg yolks
   2 egg whites, beaten with 2 drops peppermint extract to glaze the top
   1-1/2 cups granulated white sugar
   1/2 pound butter, warmed to room temperature
   2/3 cup strong kudzu root tea, warmed to room temperature
   1/2 cup plain flour

Preparation: Combine all the ingredients, except the egg whites, and beat until smooth. Pour into a 9-inch pie shell. Glaze the top. Bake in preheated 400-degree oven for 20 minutes, or until glaze is brown. This dessert deserves its name; the taste is *divine!*

Kudzu Root Vinegar

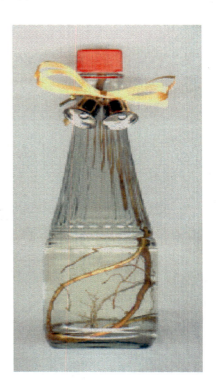

This is the easy way to make kudzu root vinegar, but it takes time. Add tender kudzu roots to white or apple cider vinegar, and set in a sunny window for about a month or two. Taste. Some roots flavor the vinegar quicker than others.

There are two ways to speed the process. One way is to cut the roots into short lengths to expose more surfaces to the vinegar. If you like the appearance of the whole root, add one as well. Shake the bottle frequently.

The second way is to bring the vinegar to a boil before pouring over the roots. The vinegar usually becomes flavored in about three weeks.

The ribbon and bells, as shown in the photograph, are not required. This bottle of kudzu root vinegar is on its way to a friend.

Bark of Kudzu Products

A $5 million dollar investment, in United States dollars, has been undertaken in China to develop a line of products from kudzu bark. Among the products under development are Cream of the Bark of Kudzu, Powder of the Bark of Kudzu, and Kudzu Vermicelli.

The statement on the Web site at http://www.hunan-window.com is: These products are refined and processed from kudzu in a scientific way, and they are not only food but also medicine. With abundant resources of kudzu, a production line will be built to expand to produce more varieties. The Chinese enterprise involved is the Zhang Jia Jie Food Processing Factory.

Make Your Own Kudzu Powder?

In 1998, a company advertised genuine, pure, made-in-America kudzu powder for sale on the Internet for $40 a pound! Having been told for years that all kudzu powder sold in the United States is imported from Japan and Korea, I was thrilled! I grabbed my credit card, pulled up the on-line order form, and ordered 2 pounds.

The total came up on the screen = $89.75 for 2 pounds of pure kudzu powder and shipping. I was directed to click to send the order. Click! Response: "Sorry, our stock is depleted but will be replenished shortly. Please check back soon."

What about back orders? I dashed off an e-mail inquiry. Reply: "Sorry, we do not accept back orders. Please check our Web site, as we will be restocking the item you ordered soon. Thank you, and we do hope you will check back."

Each time I placed an order, there was no stock. I suppose that to get rid of my questions about how they made kudzu starch, and my requests for back orders, they sent me their directions. I have read other directions, but these are in simpler language and describe the same procedures as the more verbose instructions. Here they are for any reader who wishes to give it a go. I went part of the way. Good luck to any and all who try!

Supplies: We suggest that you buy good, strong tools you can use to dig out the kudzu roots, such as a pick and shovel, if you don't already have them. Also, you will need a heavy duty sharp knife to cut the kudzu, a blender for smashing up the roots, and an old-fashioned metal washtub to soak the roots in.

The kudzu roots put heavy loads on the blender. We got ours at a restaurant supply house. We covered our soaking tubs with a very fine, but heavy, plastic mesh to keep trash out, even though it was winter. Put the tub out of reach of your pets and the squirrels.

Digging roots: During the coldest part of the winter, dig the biggest kudzu roots you can find. Don't try to make starch from any roots with a diameter of less than 1-1/2 inches.

Wash: Cut off each end, wash, and scrub what is left with a stiff brush.

I dug the kudzu roots shown in the photograph to the left. I say dig, but it was more like a wrestling match, except that it was not staged. The outcome was in doubt until the final grunt!

I washed the dirt away. Horrors! After this herculean effort, most of my roots were less than the recommended 1-1/2 inch diameter. I was too frustrated to return to the dig, and used what I had. My knife was not sharp enough to slice the roots, so I resorted to my trusty saw.

Cut: Cut the roots into piece, and slice as thin as possible. Slicing was out of the question, so I sawed as thin as possible. Truthfully, the result was not thin slices like a potato, as I had envisioned when going into this project, but a mangled mess.

Liquefy in a blender: Fill the blender half full of water. Add roots and puree. When the blender gets overloaded, add more water or remove the load and start again.

This is the way I remember my new, heavy duty blender just before it ascended into Blender Heaven!

I did not empty the blender. I just put it, and all the kudzu roots, in a plastic body bag and took it to the landfill.

About a year has passed. I have a new blender. Mercifully, I don't see any kudzu growing out of the landfill!

This experience has reduced my feelings of "being robbed" when I buy real kudzu powder! I have a greater appreciation of how hard it is to get those HUGE vines out of the earth, extract the powder, and get it across the Pacific to Tennessee. All this spells hard work and big bucks. It also made me more determined than ever to inspire someone to mine this "white gold" here in the United States. Here are the remaining steps for the stout-hearted.

Put Liquefied Roots in Water: Empty the pureed roots into a large container, such as a wash tub. Cover and let it stand outside in the cold for at least two days. It won't hurt it to freeze, but it has to thaw so it can be strained.

Strain: Strain the liquid through a sieve or cloth to remove all the root material. Fill the container back up with water and let it stand in the cold for another day.

Remove the Starch: The starch will be on the bottom in a kind of cake. Pour off the water and scrape out the starch. It will not be white, but probably a tannish color.

Purify: Put the starch in a container and again fill with water. Let stand for one day in a cold place. Do this over and over until the starch looks white. When it is white enough to suit you, scrape it out and spread it on a clean surface to dry. Cover lightly with a cloth and let it dry for about six weeks. After it is dry, seal in airtight jars. It will keep for years.

This e-mail came after *the dig.* In response to your question as to how many roots we use to get a pound of starch, we dug a regular washtub full and got about 20 ounces. You have to cut the ends off so there is a lot of waste. Dig more than you think you will want.

Last e-mail: Making kudzu starch was a fun project. We went on the Internet before we had an ample supply. We have decided to stop making starch except for our own use, and are taking down our Web site. Good luck!!!

Personal Observation: I think the Web owners read a book, got dollars in their eyes, put up the Web site, and never could make starch, but were too embarrassed to say so!!!!

Part IV
Kudzu Vine Powder®

I developed Kudzu Vine Powder®. It is a pure 100% kudzu powder made from dried kudzu vines, leaves, flowers and roots. Kudzu seed pods are leathery so they are not used. Kudzu Vine Powder® is a convenient way to enjoy the flavor and nutrients of kudzu all year round. The exact contents of Kudzu Vine Powder® are not in the public domain. However, I am happy to share the basic concept, instructions for making your own version of kudzu vine powder, and recipes for using it.

Kudzu Vine Powder® is not to be confused with the starch extracted from mature kudzu roots. That extraction is sold commercially under the names "Kudzu Powder," "Kudzu Root Powder," "Kudzu Root Starch," "Kudzu Starch," and "Kudzu Flour."

Equipment Needed to Make Kudzu Vine Powder

1. Dried kudzu vines, leaves, flowers, tender roots.

For the best flavor, and highest nutritional value, combine a quantity of each of these kudzu parts. If all of them are not available at the same time, make the powder from what you have, and add to it when other kudzu becomes available.

2. An electric mill designed to pulverize plant material to a fine powder. If you do not have this type of mill, be sure to check the specifications before you buy, because some are designed to reduce plant material to granules, not powder. This is especially true of the hand-powered mills and grinders.

This photograph shows the mill I have used about 20 years to grind everything from peppercorns to kudzu. It has about 1/2 cup capacity and is lightning fast.

3. Scissors

4. A sifter

5. A large container to hold the sifter

6. Spoons

7. Dry towels

8. Airtight jars for storing the Kudzu Vine Powder

Harvesting Kudzu for Kudzu Vine Powder

Before harvesting kudzu, decide the most convenient method to dry it. The best method I have found is a room with good air circulation, and space to spread the kudzu out of direct sunlight. I have tried drying kudzu outside, in a conventional oven, a microwave oven, and a food dehydrator, but none produced as good results as room drying. You may have better success! The goal is to produce dried kudzu which is clean and free of insects.

Kudzu to be dried is best when harvested on a sunny morning after the dew has evaporated. Harvest vines from the tip to the point where the cluster of three leaves is no more than 6 inches in diameter. Leaves in clusters over six inches are generally tough. Snipping in lengths of 1 foot or less makes the kudzu easier to handle and speeds the drying process.

If you cut leaves from the vine, snip them below the cluster of three leaves. Loose leaves are hard to handle.

Harvest the entire kudzu raceme (main stem) if it has open flowers.

Do not harvest any kudzu that is wilted, discolored, or hosting insects.

This photograph shows an ideal kudzu root from which to harvest small, tender roots. Bypass the woody roots, such as the split ones shown the photograph.

Drying Kudzu for Powdering

Kudzu must be dried as soon as possible to prevent mildew. Wash thoroughly and drain. Spread in a single layer to dry to the touch. Snip all the kudzu — vines, leaves, flowers, roots — into 1/2 to 1-inch lengths, and spread in a single layer to dry. The green kudzu is much easier to snip than dry kudzu, and far less messy. If your powdering machine will powder lengths longer than 1 inch, snip to that length. After the kudzu has dried for two or three days, cover with a thin cloth to keep it in place.

The Greeks used the lovely word *aromata* to cover all that we call spices, herbs, perfume, drugs and incense. During the drying period, *aromata* will float through the air!

Drying time varies, but the minimum for room drying is about two weeks. A simple test will tell you if the kudzu is dry enough to process into kudzu vine powder. Rub leaves and flowers between your fingers. If you hear a crackle, or if they flake, they are ready. Break a vine, and it will snap if thoroughly dried. The roots are harder to test, so I put a few in the mill and grind. If I get powder, they are ready. Everything must be extremely dry before you can powder efficiently.

If it is not convenient to make kudzu vine powder when the kudzu is sufficiently dry, store it in airtight jars. Kudzu is hydroscopic (absorbs moisture from the air) and therefore keeps best when stored in airtight containers away from hot temperature and light.

Making Kudzu Vine Powder

Assemble your equipment in a dry area. Follow the directions for the mill you are using, and powder the kudzu. Pour into the sifter, and sift into the container. There will almost always be granules in the sifter, as shown in these photographs. From left to right are shown kudzu vines and leaves, kudzu flowers, and kudzu roots after the first grinding.

Return the granules to the grinder and powder again. This is generally more efficient than attempting to powder the whole load. If there are granules after reasonable grinding, discard. The photograph below shows Kudzu Vine Powder®.

When all the kudzu is powdered, mix to distribute the powder from the leaves, vines, flowers, and roots as evenly as possible. The color of kudzu vine powder will vary with the quantity of vines, leaves, flowers and roots powdered into the mixture. Store in sterilized, dry, airtight jars in a cool, dry place. High temperature and light cause deterioration.

Cooking with Kudzu Vine Powder

Spicy Red Potatoes

Ingredients:
8 large red skinned potatoes
1 large, mild dry onion
1 tablespoon Kudzu Vine Powder
1 teaspoon salt
1/2 teaspoon black pepper

Preparation:
Cut potatoes into 1-inch cubes
Chop onion finely
Saute potatoes until they clear. Add onion and seasonings. Saute until onion clears. Spread on a cookie sheet. Bake uncovered at 250 degrees in preheated oven 30 minutes.

Kudzu Vine Powder Bread in a Bread Machine

This loaf of bread was made in the Panasonic bread machine I have enjoyed for almost 11 years.

I used a recipe for a basic loaf of bread, added 1/2 cup of chopped, dried kudzu blossoms, and followed the directions for the machine. I have added kudzu vine powder to whole wheat and rye bread recipes with excellent results.

The addition of kudzu vine powder to prepared bread-machine mixes produced a well risen loaf with good texture.

South of the Mason-Dixon Line Chili

Ingredients:
1 pound lean, ground beef
2 cups peeled diced tomatoes in natural juice
1 cup cooked kidney beans
1/4 cup kudzu vine powder
1 small onion, minced
1 tablespoon chili powder, or adjust to taste; salt and pepper optional.

Preparation:
Saute beef in a cooking pot. Add the other ingredients. Cover and simmer over low heat for a minimum of 3 hours. Stir occasionally. It's better when heated next day.

Pork Roast

3-pound pork loin roast
Marinate the roast for at least
10 hours in:
1/2 cup soy sauce
3 cups apple juice
1/2 cup Kudzu Vine Powder
If this quantity does not cover
the roast, turn the roast during
marinating or prepare more

marinade. Remove from marinade and saute to seal. Preheat the oven to 325 degrees. Place in a covered pan and bake for 1 hour. Uncover and cook 1/2 hour. Cut through the center. If there is any pink, return to oven and bake until you can be sure the whole roast is well cooked. Glaze the roast with raspberry jelly, slice and serve.

Kudzu Vine Powder Salad Dressing

3/4 cup white vinegar
1/2 cup safflower oil - or your favorite oil
1/4 cup honey or syrup
1/4 cup orange juice

1/4 cup toasted Kudzu Vine Powder
1 teaspoon salt
1 teaspoon black or white pepper
3 tablespoons chopped pimiento

Place the Kudzu Vine Powder in a thin layer in a 400-degree oven for 5 minutes, and let cool before using. This is not necessary, but some persons prefer the cooked taste.

Blend the liquid items in a blender until completely mixed and smooth. Add the dry ingredients and blend for 2-3 minutes on high. Add the chopped pimiento and whirl for a few seconds. Stop while the red color is still visible. Let stand at room temperature for 5 hours, then refrigerate. Makes about 16 ounces. This is also a good marinade.

Quiche — 8 Servings

1 pound sharp cheddar cheese
4 jumbo size eggs
1/2 cup chopped pecans
3/4 cup Kudzu Vine Powder
4 tablespoons milk
Salt and pepper to taste

Grate the cheese very fine. Beat the eggs slightly, and stir in the other ingredients. Pour in an unbaked pie shell, or heated, buttered pan, to bake without a crust. Bake 45 minutes, or until light brown, in a 250-degree oven.

Move Over McDonald's — Kudzuburger is Here!

Ingredients for the Kudzuburger:
  1 pound ground beef
  1/4 cup kudzu vine powder
  1 teaspoon salt,
    or use onion salt
  1 teaspoon black pepper
  1 tablespoon sugar

**Suggestions for Garnish —
    but anything goes:**
  Cheese, lettuce, tomato,
  pickle slices, onion, mustard,
  ketchup, mayonnaise

Preparation:
Combine all the ingredients in a bowl and stir well. Refrigerate for a minimum of 4 hours, but overnight is preferable to allow the beef time to absorb the flavors from the spices. Shape into patties. Fry in a heavy skillet, or on a grill, until well done.

Serve:
On your favorite types of rolls.

Meat Loaf with Melody Sauce

Use the Kudzuburger recipe to make a meat loaf. Serve with Melody Sauce, so named because it is to meat loaf what melody is to music.

Ingredients for 2-1/2 cups Melody Sauce:
4 ounces of very good quality aged Cheddar cheese. This is essential, because only aged cheese melts without becoming stringy.
  2 cups whole milk
  1 egg yolk; whip slightly and add to the milk
  1/4 cup kudzu vine powder
  9 tablespoons all-purpose flour
  6 tablespoons butter
  1/4 teaspoon Worcestershire sauce
  Salt and pepper to suit your preference, and add a dash of cayenne pepper

Preparation:
Melt the butter over low heat, add the flour and cook for 3 minutes. Add the milk with the whipped egg yolk. Stir constantly until the mixture thickens. Add the remaining ingredients and stir to mix, simmer for 4-5 minutes, then remove from heat. The sauce has a more developed flavor if allowed to cool and heated when ready to serve.

Melody Sauce can be kept for up to 5 days if stored in an airtight container in the refrigerator. Reheat over low heat before serving, and stir thoroughly at intervals.